Roads and Curves Ahead

A Trip Through Time with Classic Kansas City Star Quilt Blocks

By Edie McGinnis

KANSAS CITY STAR BOOKS

Roads and Curves Ahead
A Trip Through Time with Kansas City Star Quilts

By Edie McGinnis
Edited by Doug Worgul
Blocks photographed by Tim Janicke
Quilts photographed by Bill Krzyzanowski
Book design and production by River City Studio

Published by KANSAS CITY STAR BOOKS
1729 Grand Boulevard
Kansas City, Missouri, USA 64108

First edition

Library of Congress Control Number:
2002110355

ISBN: 0-9722739-2-1

Printed in the United States of America
By Walsworth Publishing Co.

To order copies call StarInfo, (816) 234-4636

For more information about this and other fine
books from Kansas City Star Books visit our Web
site at http://thekansascitystore.com or visit
www.pickledish.com.

Dedication

This book is dedicated to my three sons, Casey, Michael and Joey McGinnis. I am long overdue in thanking them for their patience. I have dragged them into countless quilt shops and to quilt shows over the years and they have graciously tolerated my passion. Thanks guys! I love you.

Acknowledgements

Thanks first to Peggy Hutinett of Raytown, Missouri, for writing and contributing her wonderful "Road Wisdom" verses for the "Burma Shave"-style signs in this book. What a great friend!

Many thanks go to the people who made the blocks and tested the patterns. I couldn't do these books without these folks, Sharon McMillan (my big sister), Marquette Heights, Illinois, Peggy McFeeters, Morton, Illinois, Sue McNamara, Viv Browning and Debbie Pulley, Peoria, Illinois, Krys Reese of Independence, Missouri; My "rowdy friends" Ruby Downing, Oak Grove, Missouri, Corky and Peggy Hutinett and Karlene Cooper of Raytown, Missouri, Rita Briner, Lee's Summit, Missouri, Clara Diaz, Brenda Butcher, Rosemary Garten, Dee Clevenger, Linda Kriesel, Donna English and Judy Lovell all of Independence, Missouri.

Special thanks to Brenda Butcher, Dee Clevenger, Karlene Cooper, Corky and Peggy Hutinett and Clara Diaz for their help in putting the sampler quilt together in time to get it photographed for the book. Karlene opened her home for a couple of days while we put the quilt together and for her generosity. I am most grateful. Corky and Peggy also lent a marvelous camel-back trunk to use as a prop.

I owe Rita Briner of Quilter's Station in Lee's Summit, Missouri, a big thank you for all her encouragement and support.

I appreciate and am encouraged by the many responses to our request for quilts to photograph for this book. I am grateful to all the quilt owners who were willing to share their lovely quilts with us.

Thanks also to Tim Janicke and Bill Krzyzanowski, our photographers and Mendy Kling of River City Studio for her wonderful design work, and finally, my editor, Doug Worgul, for his patience, encouragement and understanding.

I especially want to thank Judy Strue for lending us some wonderful antique props and for sharing her quilts.

Most of all, I want to thank Casey, Michael and Joey for providing me with so many meaningful and delightful memories to write about, and for their patience.

Table of Contents

About the Author

Edie McGinnis has been quilting for over 25 years. She is a member of the American Quilter's Society, the Quilters Guild of Greater Kansas City, and the Calico Cut-ups Quilting Club of Independence, Missouri. This is the fifth quilt book Edie has written about *The Kansas City Star* quilt patterns. She has taught quilting classes and given lectures about *The Star* quilt patterns.

Roads and Curves Ahead

The names of quilt patterns have always intrigued me. As I rummage through some of the classic patterns that have been published by The Kansas City Star, I sometimes get bogged down pondering how certain patterns ended up with their particular names. I'm sure some of the names have been appended because the patterns resembled items such as the "Smoothing Iron" or the "Anvil" or "Patty's Summer Parasol." I suspect a lot of patterns got their names because some woman was on the road. It probably was not her choice either. I imagine she was trudging along beside a husband who was filled with expectations of new beginnings.

For me though, the names of the patterns in this book evoke memories of vacations and day trips. Some I took with my dad and mom and some I took with my children. One of the ways we entertained ourselves while riding in the car when I was a child, was by reading the Burma Shave signs posted along the roadsides. Of course, those were gone by the time I had children but what fun they were.

I reared three boys, Casey, Michael and Joey. We had two major rules when we went on vacations. Rule number one – no fighting in the car. Rule number two – we stop whenever one person wants to stop. Sometimes it is difficult to keep children from bickering in the car. When that happened, the refrain that gritted through my clenched jaw was, "Don't make me stop this car. If I have to stop this car, we are going back home."

Now my boys are grown. One is married, one soon will be married and the youngest is trying to figure out what kind of a career would suit him. To a man though, they talk about vacation memories. Along with the laughing and joking that goes with the reminiscing, the phrase, "Don't make me stop this car." invariably pops out of someone's mouth. I can't wait until they have children of their own!

As you peruse these patterns, think about your own memories. Share the laughter and the fun you've had with your family and friends and turn the memories into a quilt. I've even thrown you a few curves. After all, that's what life is all about, going down the roads of our lives and dealing with the stumbling blocks and curves. Later on we add the laughter.

There are nine patterns in this book requiring curved seams. Some are gradual curves and some are pretty tight. Here are a few suggestions that will make your life a little easier when dealing with these curves.

Take the path of least resistance. If you find it easier to piece the block and then applique a circle where it is needed, by all means do so. The quilt police will not put you in jail for this.

After cutting any curved pieces, fold them in half and finger press them along the fold. Align the two creases and pin at that juncture as well as at the beginning and the end of the seam. Three pins should be sufficient. Sew slowly and align the raw edges as you go.

Clipping the fabric about 1/8th of an inch every so often along the concave edge is also helpful in making the seams lie flat. It is not necessary to clip the convex side.

Generally speaking, it is easier to hand piece curves while holding the concave side closest to you.

Please remember that these are just guidelines and not rules. Do what is most comfortable for you.

Road to Arkansas made by Karlene Cooper of Raytown, Missouri.

Her family's fed
and gone to bed,

The clock strikes
half-past one.

Her eyes are red,
her arms like lead,

But her quilt
at last is done.

K. C. STAR QUILTS!

My friend, Krys Reese, helped her daughter, Kassandra, and son-in-law, Randy, move from California to Missouri about two years ago. Kassandra was six months pregnant at the time so she and Krys drove the car while Randy and Kassandra's best friend, Irena, drove a rental truck. The truck moved at a faster pace than the car due to frequent car stops caused by Baby-on-the-Bladder Syndrome. The vehicles would catch up with each other at the end of the day so they could start out together the next morning.

When the moving truck crossed the state line into Texas, it was surrounded by highway patrol cars with flashing lights and forced to pull off onto a country road. The police officers asked Randy and Irena to produce the vehicle papers and their driver's licenses. Randy had a California license and Irena's was from Illinois. The police seemed perturbed about that.

More problematic was that the police wanted to know what was in the truck. The papers stated it was furniture. Hmmmm. Moving truck — furniture. It all seemed pretty obvious. But the officers insisted on looking in the back of the truck and ordered Randy and Irena to open the doors. The lock on the doors was a combination lock and Kassandra was the only one who knew the combination.

The police were about to cut the lock off the door when Irena told them she worked for the State of Illinois and showed her identification badge. The police then let them go on their way.

Outside of Liberal, Kansas, they were stopped again. Police again wanted to inspect the truck's contents. This time Krys and Kassandra were right behind the truck. They pulled over and Kassandra began to waddle up to the truck. The officer ordered her to stay back. He apparently thought she was dangerous, armed as she was with a cell phone and protruding stomach.

They later learned that they had been stopped because trucks from this particular rental company had reportedly been used for purposes other than furniture moving. Several vans from this company had been stopped in New Mexico and Texas loaded with illegal aliens.

Journey to California

12" Finished Block
1955

Fabric needed: light, medium light, medium and dark.

From EACH fabric, cut one 2" square or use template D, one triangle using template E, one triangle using template B, one triangle using template C and one triangle using template A.

NOTE: Color placement is what this block is all about. Lay all the pieces out before sewing to get the correct effect.

Sew the four squares together as shown.

Add the E triangles next.

Now add the B triangles.

Next stitch the C triangles in place as shown.

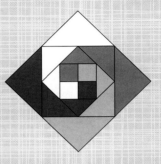

To complete the block, add the large A triangles. Your block should look like this.

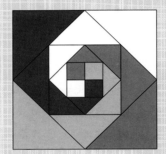

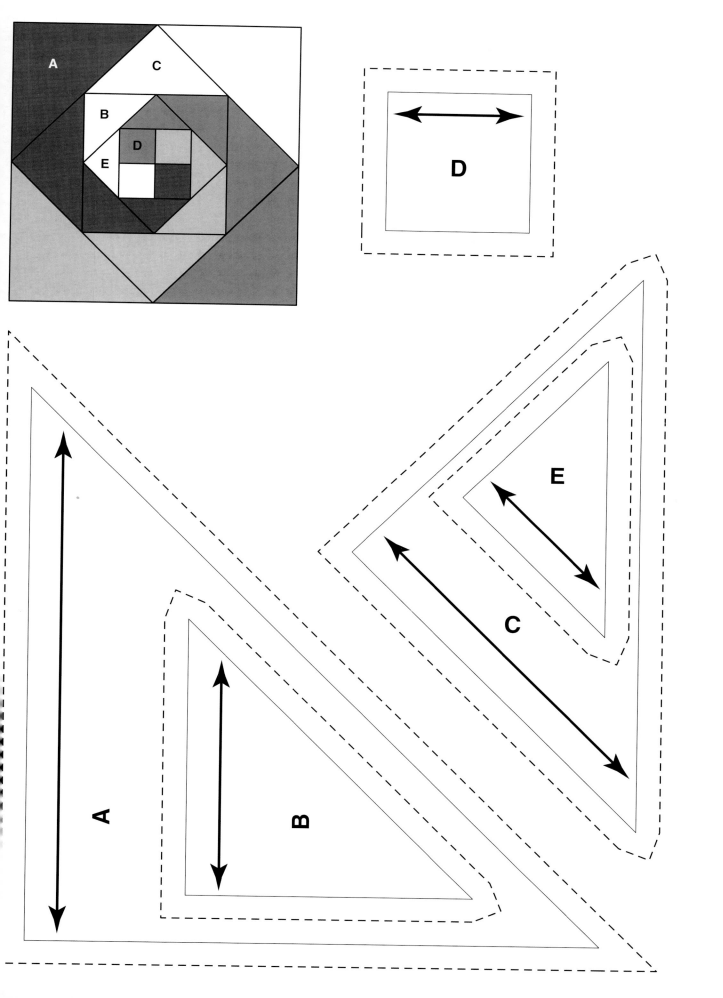

A

B

C

D

E

Chisholm Trail made by Debbie Pulley of Peoria, Illinois.

When you view someone's quilt

Hanging in a show,

Be careful of your comments,

And always keep them low.

K. C. STAR QUILTS!

Back in 1865, a trader named Jesse Chisholm made his way from San Antonio, Texas, to Abilene, Kansas. He followed the traces of a trail made by retreating federal soldiers nearly four years earlier. Cattle ranchers then followed his route and drove their herds through Oklahoma Indian Territory to the railheads in Kansas.

Back in 1997, the boys and I went to the Mike Murphy cattle drive in downtown Kansas City. For readers unfamiliar with this relatively new Kansas City tradition here's an explanation. The event began in 1996 when local radio personality Mike Murphy organized it as a way to celebrate the 100th anniversary of the last real cattle drive in Kansas City. It's been held every year since except for the year 2000. The cowboys let the cattle out of the corral and drive them through part of the city. Hopefully, all goes well and the cattle cooperate and go where they are supposed to go.

That seldom happens.

The year the boys and I went, several of the cattle wandered away from the herd and had to be chased down by some of the cowboys. Some of the cows were found in front of City Hall. Some had wandered into a parking garage and ended up on the eighth floor. And one ornery bovine chased a startled motorcycle policeman.

One spectator standing near us was obviously from out of town and disapproved of the whole proceeding. We heard him remark, "Well, you certainly wouldn't see anything like this going on in Boston."

Chisholm Trail

12" Finished Block
1939

Fabric needed: light, medium and dark.

From the light fabric, cut seven 3 7/8" squares or cut 14 triangles using template A.

From the medium fabric, cut seven 3 7/8" squares or cut 14 triangles using template A.

From the dark fabric, cut two 3 1/2" squares or use template B.

For this block you will need to make 14 half-square triangle units. To make the half-square triangles, draw a diagonal line from corner to corner on the reverse side of the light 3 7/8" squares.

Place each light 3 7/8" square on top of a medium 3 7/8" square with the right sides of the fabric facing each other. Stitch 1/4" from the line on either side of the line.

Cut along the line, open each unit and press the seam allowance to the darkest side of the fabric. You should have fourteen half-square triangle units.

To construct the block, sew four half-square triangle units together as shown for the first row.

For the next row, sew two half-square triangle units together, and then add a dark square followed by another half-square triangle unit. This row should look like this.

The third row consists of one half-square triangle unit sewn to a dark square with two more half-square triangles added. The row should look like this.

The final row has the remaining four half-square triangle units sewn together as shown.

Sew the four rows together to complete the block. It should look like this.

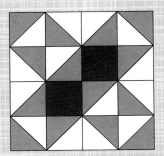

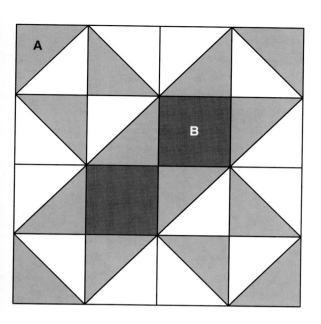

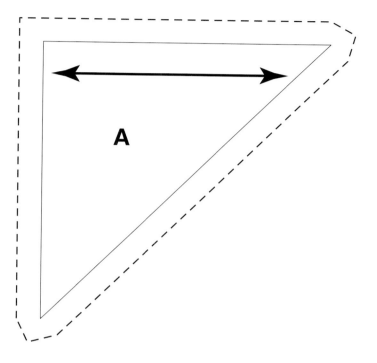

A

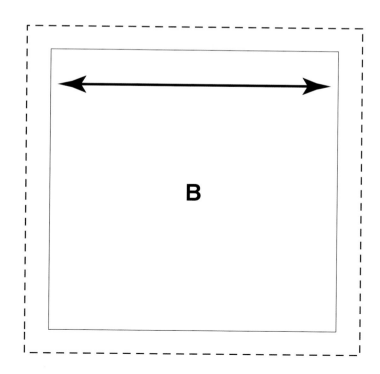

B

Crossroads made by Rita Briner of Quilter's Station, Lee's Summit, Missouri.

If you keep your work space

Tidy, clean and neat,

You won't be finding needles

In your stocking feet.

K. C. STAR QUILTS!

After my sons Casey and Michael left home, Joey and I were on our own for vacations. When he was just about to turn 16 years old, we flew to California. It was Joe's first time on an airplane and he had never seen the ocean.

We landed at the Santa Barbara airport where my friends, Ann and Bill met us. The airport is small and beautifully landscaped. The Bird-of-Paradise were blooming along with a multitude of other flowers. We had left snow on the ground in Kansas City.

We spent a week sightseeing during the day and playing rummy at night. Joe spent one day at a roller blade park that had all sorts of jumps and curved walls. He was in his element.

Before we left we went to the ocean. There is an old superstition that says, "If you dip your feet in the ocean, you'll come back to California." We took our shoes and socks off and Joe and I went wading in the icy water. My baggy-jeaned son and I sat on a log and dried our feet with our socks and I wondered how many more of these moments Joey and I would have.

Crossroads
12" Finished Block
1931

Fabric needed: light, medium and dark.

NOTE: You will need to cut reverse pieces for this block. To do this, either flip the template over or fold your fabric and cut through both layers of fabric at once.

From the light fabric, cut four strips using template A, one square using template E, four pieces using template C and four pieces using template Cr.

From the medium fabric, cut four pieces using template D.

From the dark fabric, cut four pieces using template B and four pieces using template Br.

Sew each of the dark B pieces to the light C pieces. We'll call these the B-C units.

Then sew the dark Br pieces to the light Cr pieces. We'll call these the Br-Cr units.

Now sew a B-C unit to one side of the D piece. Add a Br-Cr unit to the opposing side as shown.

Make four of these wedge shapes.

Sew a light A strip to two sides of the light E square.

You are now ready to construct the block. Sewing this block on the diagonal is the easiest way to put it together.

Sew a wedge shaped unit to opposing sides of an A strip as shown.

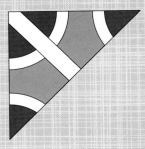

Sew the remaining two wedges to opposing sides of the remaining A strip.

Sew each of these portions to opposing sides of the center strip to complete the block.

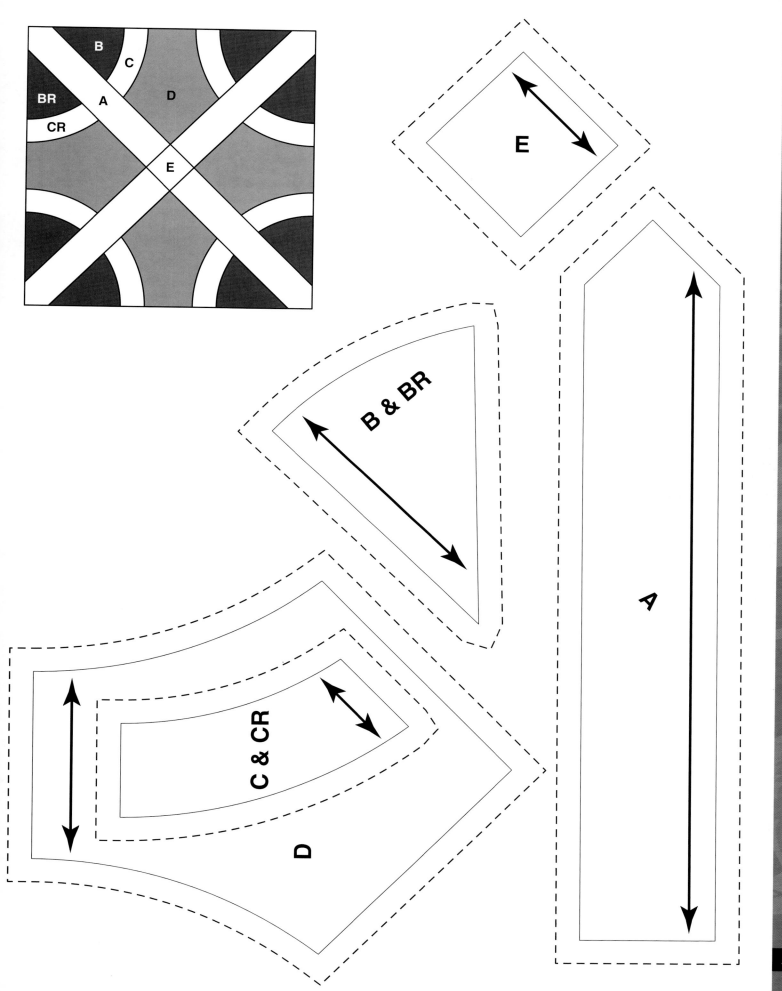

B

C

BR

A

CR

D

E

E

B & BR

A

C & CR

D

Drunkard's Path made by Clara Diaz of Independence, Missouri.

Drunkard's Path

When you're stitching curves,

And you just can't seem to win,

Here is the answer...

Pin, pin, pin.

K. C. STAR QUILTS!

One year The Star gave me a bonus of four tickets to Disney World. So that next June we were off to Florida.

We loved Disney World's Epcot. There was something there for each of us to enjoy. Joey loved the animals, especially the flamingos, Michael couldn't get enough of the computer exhibit and Casey was wild about the laser light show at the end of the day.

From Florida we headed to New Orleans. Thirty years before, when my mother and I had visited the city, we had driven across the Lake Ponchatrain bridge and I now wanted my boys to see that amazing bridge and experience the Big Easy.

We stayed in the French Quarter and had dinner on a balcony overlooking Bourbon Street. We walked all over the French Quarter, avoiding other tourists who were staggering out of the many taverns. We visited a voodoo shop, watched little boys tap dancing on the street corners while spinning a bicycle wheel on top of their heads and we listened to wonderful music rolling out of the doorways. Then we picked up Mardi Gras beads off the street after a parade passed by. It seems that every day is Mardi Gras in New Orleans, no matter what time of the year you visit.

Drunkard's Path

12" Finished Block
1959

Fabric needed: light and dark.

From the light fabric, cut eight pieces using template A and eight pieces using template B.

From the dark fabric, cut eight pieces using template A and eight pieces using template B.

Sew the light A pieces to the dark B pieces. You should have eight units that look like this.

Sew the dark A pieces to the light B pieces, making a total of eight units.

Stitch four units together to make the top row of the block, positioning the pieces as shown.

Sew the second row together as shown.

Row three is sewn together like this.

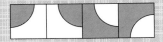

Row four is sewn with the pieces positioned as follows.

Sew the four rows together to complete the block. It should look like this.

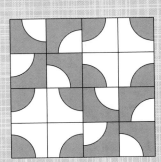

20

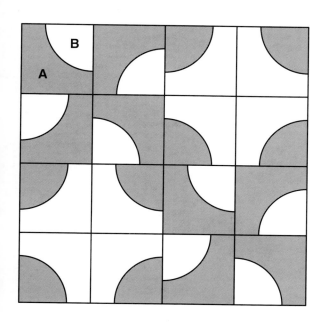

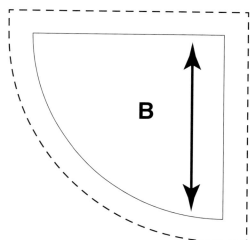

B

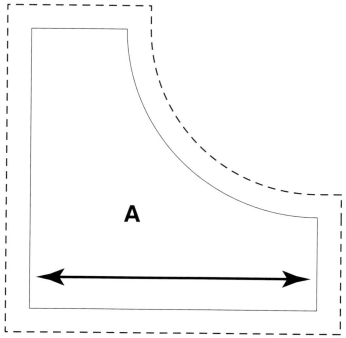

A

1930 Road to Oklahoma made by Linda Kriesel of Independence, Missouri.

Road to Oklahoma

A sign upon the Pearly Gates

Would surely make me tremble,

If I read words that said,

"Did you bring your thimble?"

K. C. STAR QUILTS!

When I was twenty, I took my first trip to California, which was also my first airplane ride. I wore a blue dress, a white hat and white shoes. When I arrived in Los Angeles I tried to cover my fear and nervousness at my unfamiliar circumstances with a veneer of sophistication.

I actually began to enjoy myself as my small-town-girl-in-the-big-city anxiety began to ease up. In the midst of my vacation, the airline pilots decided they just weren't getting paid enough and went on strike. I had to form a Plan B in order to get home. Since my funds were limited, Plan B became a bus ride. It would take four days and three nights to get back to Illinois.

The bus traveled old Route 66, through California, Nevada, New Mexico, Texas, Oklahoma, etc. I parked myself in the corner in the back of the bus where there was a large bench seat and plenty of windows.

The first day on the bus wasn't too bad. I entertained myself with the view of cactus filled desert passing by my window and people getting on and off of the bus. It wasn't long before all the people began blurring together until one GI got on the bus and sat next to me.

His name was Bill and he had been discharged from the army. He was headed home to Oklahoma. He told me stories of growing up on a farm and I told him stories of growing up in Tremont, Illinois.

As we crossed into Oklahoma, I saw oil derricks, cattle and farmers plowing their fields. The dirt was red and I asked Bill how in the world they ever grew anything in such soil. He told me that red soil was the richest. I was just sure that was wrong. After all, in Illinois the dirt was coal black and those farmers hauled in record crops.

I made that foolish assumption when I was twenty and knew all there is to know. Since I was that age everyone somehow became a lot smarter and I realized how very much there is in this world to learn. It is a lesson I tried to keep in mind when my children reached the age when they knew it all.

Road to Oklahoma

12" Finished Block
1930

Fabric needed: light, medium and dark.

NOTE: You will need to cut reverse pieces in this block. When a reverse piece is called for, you may either flip the template over or fold your fabric and cut through both thicknesses at once.

From the light fabric, cut two 3 1/2" squares or use template B, two A pieces and 2 Ar.

From the medium fabric, cut 2 triangles using template C and one piece using template A and one piece using template Ar.

From the dark fabric, cut four 3 1/2" squares or use template B.

To construct the block, sew a 4-patch unit for the center using 2 light and 2 dark 3 1/2" squares.

Sew a medium C triangle to a light Ar.

Sew this strip to the top of the 4-patch unit.

Sew a medium C triangle to a light A piece.

Add a dark square to the light end of the strip.

Now add this to the right side of the center 4-patch. Your block should now look like this.

Next sew a light and a medium A piece together and add this strip to the left side of the block.

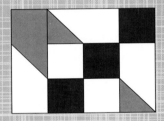

Sew the dark 3 1/2" (B) square to the remaining light Ar piece. Then add the remaining medium Ar piece.

Sew this strip to the bottom of the block. This completes the block.

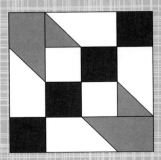

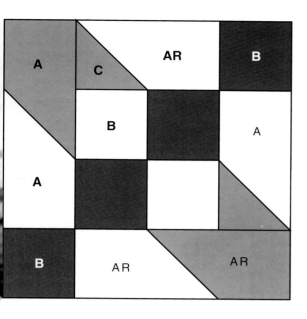

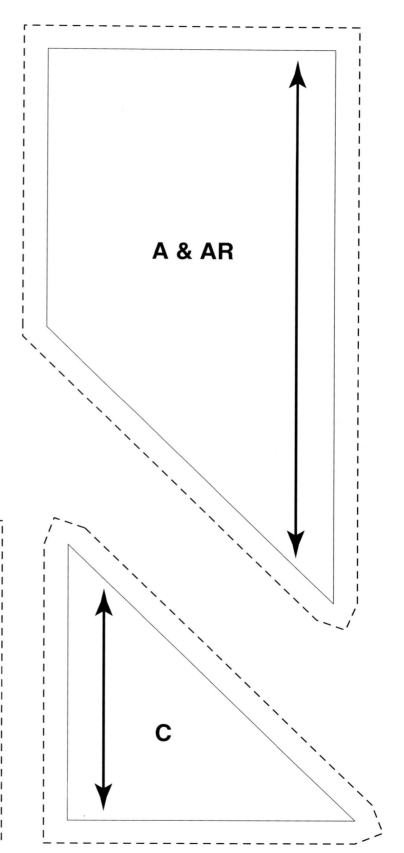

A & AR

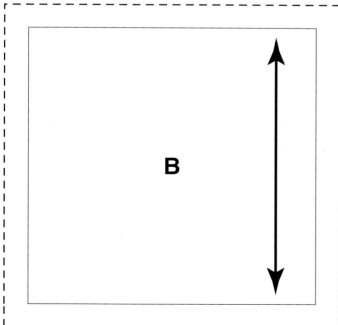

B

C

Wild Goose Chase made by Viv Browning of Peoria, Illinois.

Wild Goose Chase

One of the first real vacations the boys and I took was to Chicago, Illinois. (A "real vacation" is defined as a trip where one does not visit and/or stay with relatives.) We planned to see the Museum of Science and Industry and the Museum of Natural History, Shedd Aquarium and the Sears tower.

We checked into a hotel that had a view of Lake Michigan and was within walking distance of the aquarium and the museums.

After dinner one evening, as we were walking back to the hotel, Joey, age 8, decided he probably could catch one of the pigeons strutting along the sidewalk. His strategy was to sneak up behind one of the birds and begin walking like one, perhaps to fool the poor pigeon into thinking that another — slightly larger — bird had joined the flock. Joey folded his arms like wings, lifted his legs high, one step at a time, puffed out his chest and pushed his chin in and out with each step. He'd get within one step of a pigeon, reach out to grab it and off it would fly. Joe's pigeon strut was, by far, the most comical entertainment of the day.

On our last day in Chicago we went to the Sears Tower. We got in our car and headed in the general direction of the building. I didn't know the address of the tower, so I told the kids to keep watching, making sure we kept it in our sights.

We got closer and the building was looming large, so we decided to park the car and walk the rest of the way. We walked four blocks, then five, soon we were up to about twelve and we didn't seem to be getting any closer. Finally we asked some passersby how far we were from the Sears tower. They grinned and said, "Oh probably three or four more miles ought to get you there."

We went back to the car and, following the directions the people had given us, only got lost two more times. We finally ended our wild goose chase searching for the Sears Tower only to discover that the observation area was closed to visitors because of cloudy, rainy conditions.

Technology is marvelous.

No telling where we're headed.

But when will scientists invent

A needle that stays threaded?

K. C. STAR QUILTS!

HOTEL

CLEAN
COMFORTABLE
CONVENIENT

Wild Goose Chase

12" Finished Block
1928

Fabric needed: light, medium and dark.

From the light fabric, cut 1 square a scant 3 3/8" or use template D and 16 triangles using template A.

From the medium fabric, cut four triangles using template B.

From the dark fabric, cut 32 triangles using template C and four triangles using template A.

Sew a dark C triangle to each side of a light A triangle. This makes one flying geese unit. Make 16 of these flying geese.

Sew four flying geese together. Make four strips like this.

Now sew a flying geese strip to two sides of the light D square as shown.

Add a dark A triangle to each end of this strip.

Sew a medium B triangle to either side of each remaining flying geese strip as shown making sure all of the triangles point to the center square.

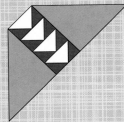

Add a dark A triangle to the corner of the flying geese units.

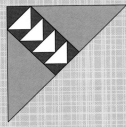

Sew the three sections together on the diagonal as shown to complete the block.

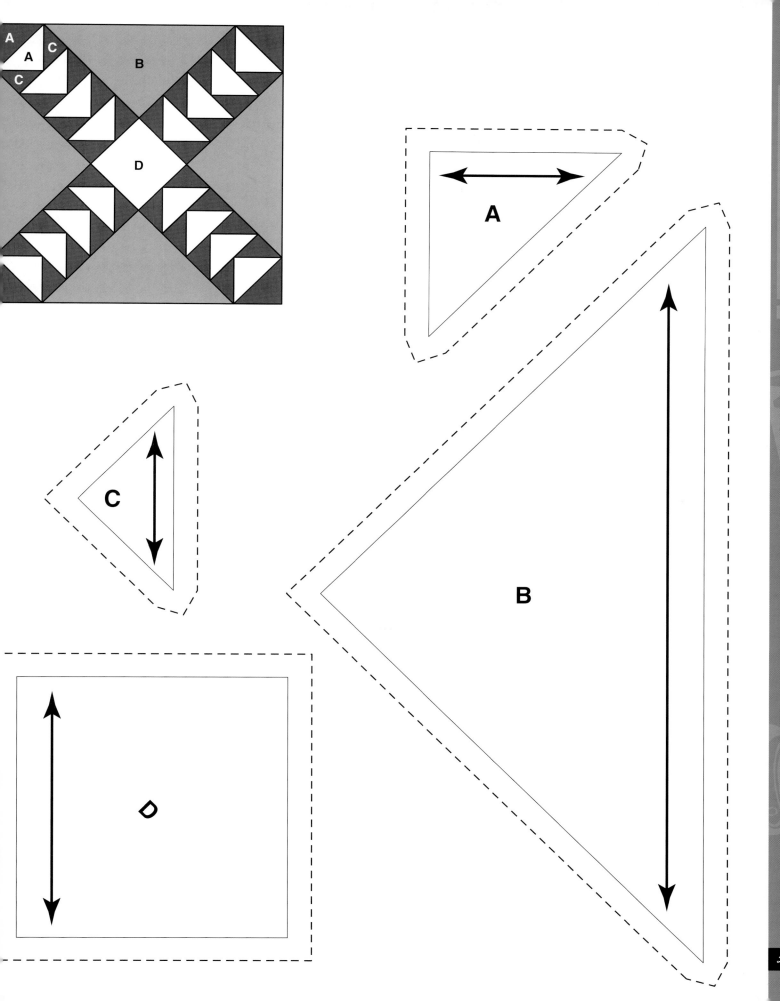

A

C

B

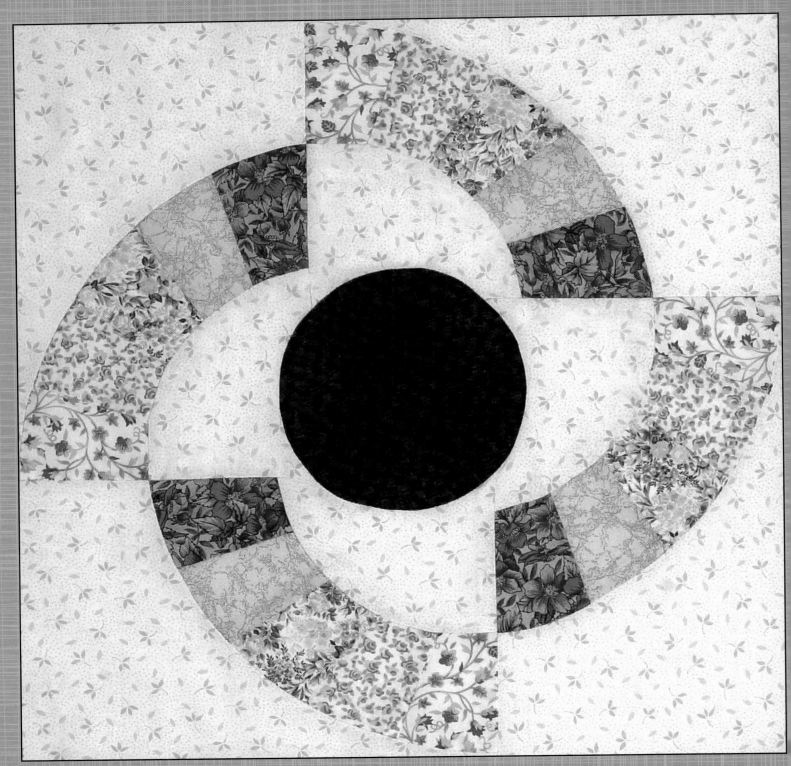

Letha's Electric Fan made by Rita Briner of Quilter's Station, Lee's Summit, Missouri.

Letha's Electric Fan

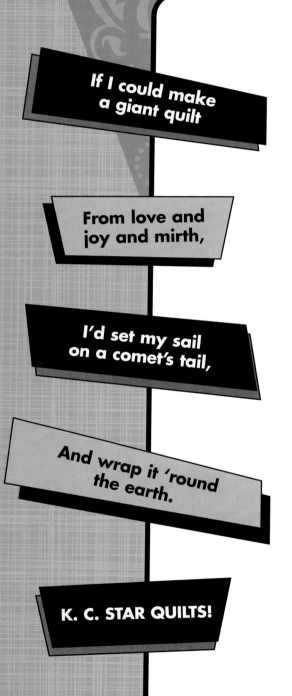

If I could make
a giant quilt

From love and
joy and mirth,

I'd set my sail
on a comet's tail,

And wrap it 'round
the earth.

K. C. STAR QUILTS!

When I was a kid, air conditioning was rare. Certainly, none of the houses in my hometown had it. In fact, we sometimes slept outside because it was so blooming hot. My grandma's porch was one of the best places to sleep outdoors, because you didn't have to worry about creepy crawly things.

Grandpa's car had the next best thing to air conditioning — a little four-bladed fan mounted on the dash of his car next to the wing window. The fan was adjustable and could be turned to face the windshield — in which case it would serve as a defroster — or toward the driver to serve as a cooling device.

On hot summer Sundays my grandma would ride to church fanning herself with a cardboard fan that featured a funeral home advertisement on the back. I would sit between them in the front seat and my grandpa would point that little fan at my face while perspiration ran down his forehead.

Letha's Electric Fan

12" Finished Block
1938

Fabric needed: light, dark and assorted prints.

From the light fabric, cut four pieces using template C and four pieces using template A. When cutting the pieces for template A, it is a good idea to cut the outside edges larger than necessary. That makes the block easy to square up when finished.

From the prints, cut four pieces using templates D, E, F, G and H.

From the dark fabric, cut one circle using template B.

Sew pieces D, E, F, G and H together. Add a light C piece. Make four fan shaped units that look like this.

Add an A piece to each of the fan shaped units. Each should now look like this.

If you are hand piecing, sew the four units together leaving the last seam open. Pin this "strip" to the center circle and stitch in place. Close the last seam to complete the block. If you are piecing this on the machine, it will be easiest to applique the circle in place after closing the last seam.

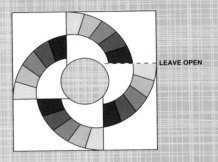

LEAVE OPEN

Trim the block to 12 1/2."

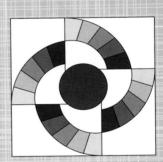

32

One of the more memorable of life's crossroads that each of my boys encountered was learning to drive. I taught each of them how to operate a stick shift with much lurching and bucking in church and school parking lots.

After they got their driver's licenses, the boys would volunteer to drive on our vacations so I could get some sleep. Hah! I couldn't close my eyes on a bet when I was sitting in the passenger seat. It always seemed like they were driving too fast or following too close. I would constantly crane my neck so I could look at the speedometer.

I tried hard not to criticize, but wasn't successful. As our car would close in on a car ahead of us, the boy behind the wheel would hear me loudly sucking my breath in through my teeth.

I don't know how they put up with me during this period of their lives. I am ashamed to admit that I still do that hissing thing when I get in the car with them. Of course, now they are old enough to pay me back with their own hissing noises when I'm driving. Since I've figured out just how annoying and nerve wracking that behavior is, I guess we can stop now. Okay, guys? Okay?

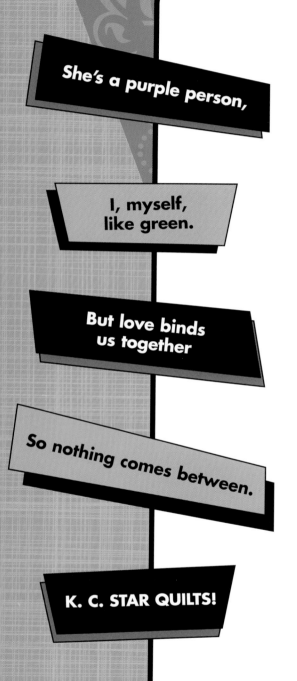

She's a purple person,

I, myself, like green.

But love binds us together

So nothing comes between.

K. C. STAR QUILTS!

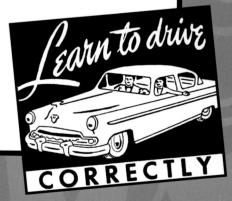

Learn to drive CORRECTLY

Hazel Valley Crossraods

12" Finished Block
1934

Fabric needed: light, medium and dark.

From the light fabric, cut four squares using template A, four strips using template E, four wedges using template C and 1 square using template F.

From the medium fabric, cut four pieces using template B.

From the dark fabric, cut eight triangles using template D and four pieces using template G.

Sew a light C piece to a medium B piece. Make four of these wedge shapes.

Sew a dark D triangle to the pointed end of an E strip as shown.

Now sew a D triangle to a light A square.

Sew this to the end of the strip.

Add a dark G piece to the other end of the strip.

Make four of these corner strips.

This block is most easily sewn together when sewn on the diagonal.

Add a wedge shape to two sides of a corner strip as shown. Make two of these units.

Sew a corner strip to opposing sides of the light F square.

Sew a triangular unit to opposing sides of the center strip to complete the block.

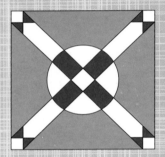

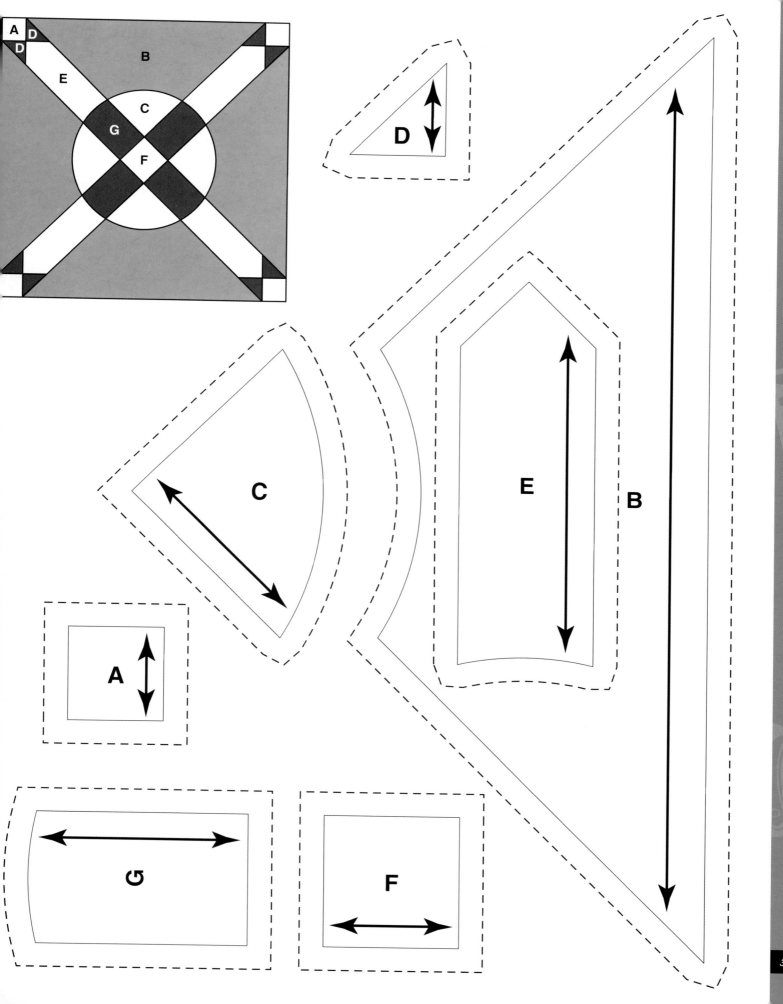

A

B

C

D

E

F

G

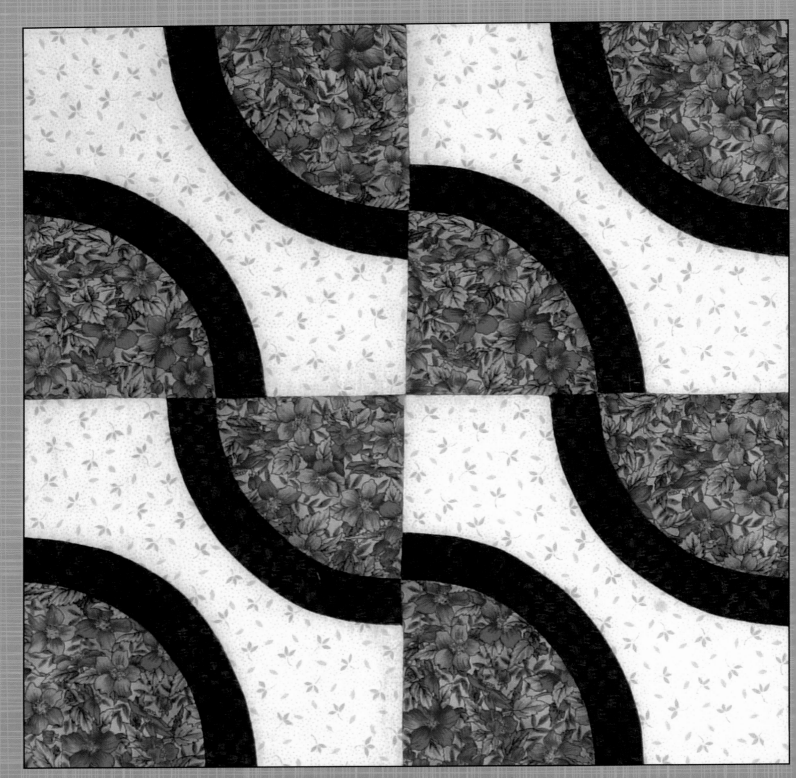

Drunkard's Trail made by Linda Kriesel of Independence, Missouri

Jacob's Ladder, Irish Chain,

Ohio Star, Sunbonnet Sue.

I can't make all the quilts I want

If I live to a hundred and two.

K. C. STAR QUILTS!

Mom was great for spur-of-the-moment trips. Before I was married, she and I both lived in Springfield, Illinois. She called me one summer day and asked if I would like to ride with her to Champaign. I agreed but when I asked about the purpose of the trip she wouldn't explain. She said she'd tell me when she picked me up.

When I got into her car, a lovely blue convertible with white leather upholstery, I again asked her why we were going to Champaign. She said we were going to get a sheep. "A sheep?" I asked, alarmed. "What do you need a sheep for? And where do you think you are going to put it? "

At the time Mom worked for the State of Illinois as a public relations specialist for Paul Powell, who was the Secretary of State. Powell had bought the grand champion wether at the State Fair. He wanted to donate the sheep to the children's petting zoo in Springfield, but someone had mistakenly sent the sheep to Champaign to be butchered. When Powell heard his sheep was to become mutton, he looked at my mom and said, "Get my sheep back."

Mom thought the sheep would be perfectly content to ride in the back seat of the car. She would just throw a blanket in the back seat and the sheep could lie down on it, nice and comfy.

We arrived at the slaughterhouse to find the sheep alive and whole. One of the workers deposited the sheep in the back of the convertible. You could tell the man thought my mom was insane. I couldn't blame him.

We headed back to Springfield. It had not occurred to my mother that the sheep would stand for the entire trip. She also had not considered the fact that the sheep was not housebroken, a fact that became increasingly evident as the sheep became increasingly stressed.

The poor sheep also was not accustomed to my mother's habit of driving with one foot on the brake and the other foot on the gas pedal. Every time Mom slammed on the brakes, the sheep fell over. It would gradually regain it's footing on the cushy seat only to fall again as mom would swerve around while passing a car. The car began to reek as our passenger expressed his displeasure.

When we reached the petting zoo the sheep staggered out of the backseat like he'd had a few too many drinks. I don't know if he ever recovered from the ride, but I know the convertible never smelled quite the same.

Drunkard's Trail

12" Finished Block
1942

Fabric needed: light, medium and dark.

From the light fabric, cut four pieces using template C.

From the medium fabric, cut eight pieces using template A.

From the dark fabric, cut 8 pieces using template B.

Sew a dark B arc to the top of each of the four light C pieces.

Add a medium A piece to the dark B arcs as shown.

Now add a B piece to the bottom of each unit. So far you should have four units, each looking like this.

Next add a medium A curved piece to each unit. They should now look like this.

Clip the curved seams and press the seam allowances toward the center of the block.

Sew the four units together as shown to complete the block.

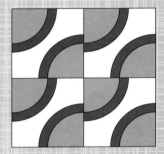

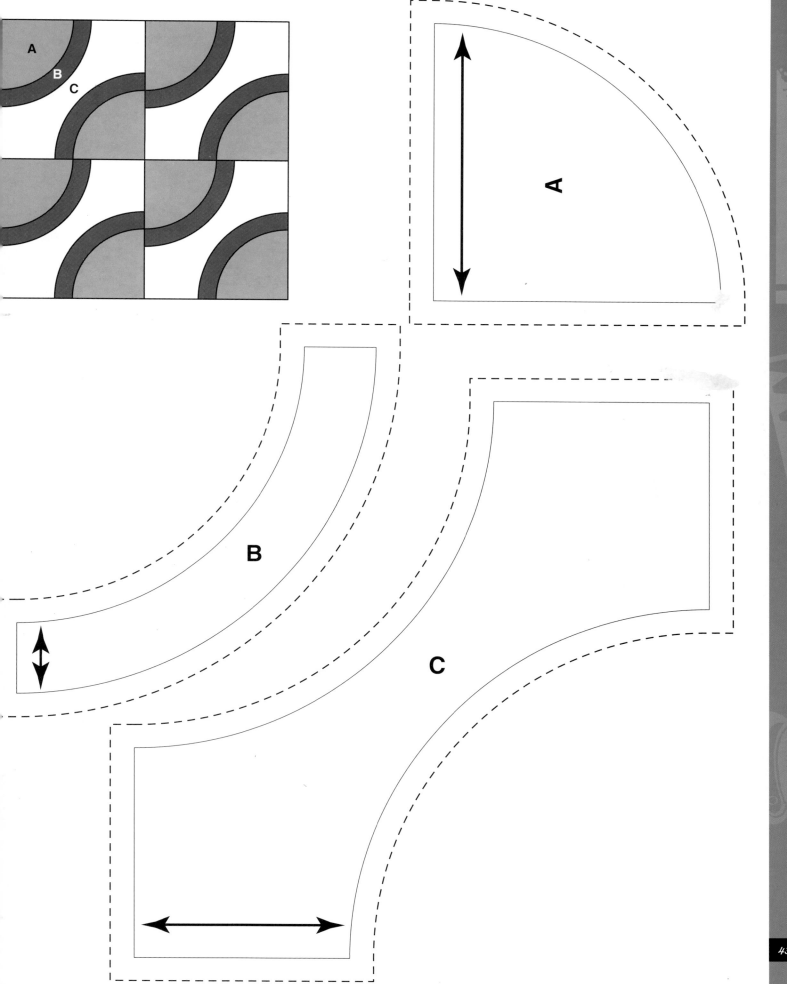

A

B

C

Roads and Curves Ahead quilted by Amber Coffey of Coffey House Quilts, Parkville, Missouri.
This is the sampler quilt one can make by using the patterns in this book.

Step into our quilt show on the following pages and enjoy the quilts others have so kindly and generously shared with us.

Clara Bolin made railroad Memories from the Railroad Crossing pattern printed in the Kansas City Star.
The quilt was started in 1985 to commemorate 40 years of railroad service by her husband, Bob,
who passed away in August of 1988. The quilt was completed in April of 1991.

This Road to Arkansas quilt was made and is owned by Sarah Abright Dickson of San Antonio, Texas.

Road to Oklahoma is owned by Joseph Frerichs and was given to him as a gift.
Grandma, Fran Frerichs of Ackley, Iowa made the quilt for Joseph just has she has for each of her grandchildren.

Wheel of Mystery was made by Corky and Peggy Hutinett of Raytown, Missouri.

Owned by Nancy Kraft of Leawood, Kansas, this Road to Oklahoma quilt was made by Nancy Jane Bruce of Buchanan County, MO more than fifty years ago.

Road to Oklahoma was made by Beverly Carpenter of Ponca City, Oklahoma.
She made it for her grandson, Andrew Pinegar, who is currently serving in the U.S. Army.

Drunkard's Path, owned by Doris Jean Arnold of Lenexa, Kansas, was made by Edna Pinnell.
It was given to Doris as a gift from her great aunt Edna when Doris was a child.

Her mother gave this Road to Arkansas quilt to Joyce Savage of Overland Park, Kansas.

Road to Arkansas owned by Judy Strue of Liberty, Missouri.

Drunkard's Path owned by Judy Strue of Liberty, Missouri.

Letha's Electric Fan, owned by Judy Strue of Liberty, Missouri. This colorful quilt was machine quilted.

Mountain Road owned by Judy Strue of Liberty, Missouri. The pattern is also called the "S" quilt.

Wheel of Mystery is owned by Judy Strue of Liberty, Missouri.
The quilt was probably made in the 30s judging from the bubblegum pink of the fabric.

Wild Goose Chase, made by Romaine Theel of Grandview, Missouri, was finished ten years ago.
It was made for her husband, a Nebraskan and avid goose hunter.

Wild Goose Chase, owned by Betty Baker of Lenexa, Kansas, was made in the 1930's
by Hattie Mae Purviance-Baker of the Rosedale area of Kansas City, Kansas.

Wheel of Mystery made by Peggy Hutinett of Raytown, Missouri.

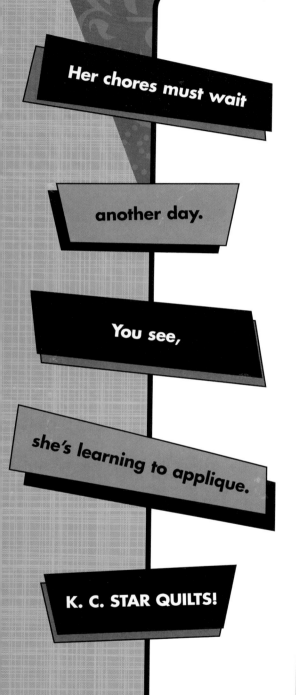

Her chores must wait

another day.

You see,

she's learning to applique.

K. C. STAR QUILTS!

When Casey and Michael were small, our family lived in Ottawa, Illinois. One of our favorite places to take the children for a picnic was Starved Rock State Park, near Utica. There were trails to wander and wildflowers to please the eyes and a scary story to tell little boys about the legend of Starved Rock.

In the 1760s, Pontiac was the chief of the Ottawa tribe. (And you thought that was a name of a car.) Pontiac was killed by an Illiniwek Indian at a tribal council in what is now southern Illinois. Of course this was not considered good diplomacy and the Ottawa Indians and the Potawatomie, their allies, vowed to avenge the killing.

A band of Illiniwek took refuge on top of a 125-foot butte after being attacked by Ottawas and Potawatomies. Though the arrows of their enemies could not reach them, the Illiniweks underestimated the patience of their enemies. The Ottawas and their compatriots surrounded the bluff and waited until the Illiniweks starved to death.

The restless ghosts of the Illiniweks are said to occupy the top of the bluff now and there are reports that sometimes you can see them drifting through the river mists.

PONTIAC
DRAMATICALLY STYLED
DYNAMICALLY POWERED

Adaption of the Indian Trail
12" Finished Block
1943

Fabric needed: light and dark.

NOTE: Since you need reverses of each piece except for D, you will want to fold your fabric and cut through both thicknesses at once.

From the light fabric, cut four A and four Ar pieces, four C and four Cr pieces.

From the dark fabric, cut four B and four Br pieces and four D pieces.

Sew a light C piece to the dark D piece. Add the Cr piece to the opposing side. Make a total of four of these. We'll call them the lower units.

Sew a light A piece to a dark B piece.

Then sew a light Ar piece to a dark Br piece.

Join the two dark pieces together as shown.

Make a total of four of these units also. We will call them the upper units.

Stitch a lower unit to an upper unit. Make a total of four that look like this. Each is one-fourth of the block.

The pieces can be sown together with the arrowheads pointing to the outside of the block or to the inside of the block.

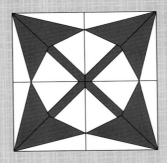 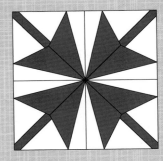

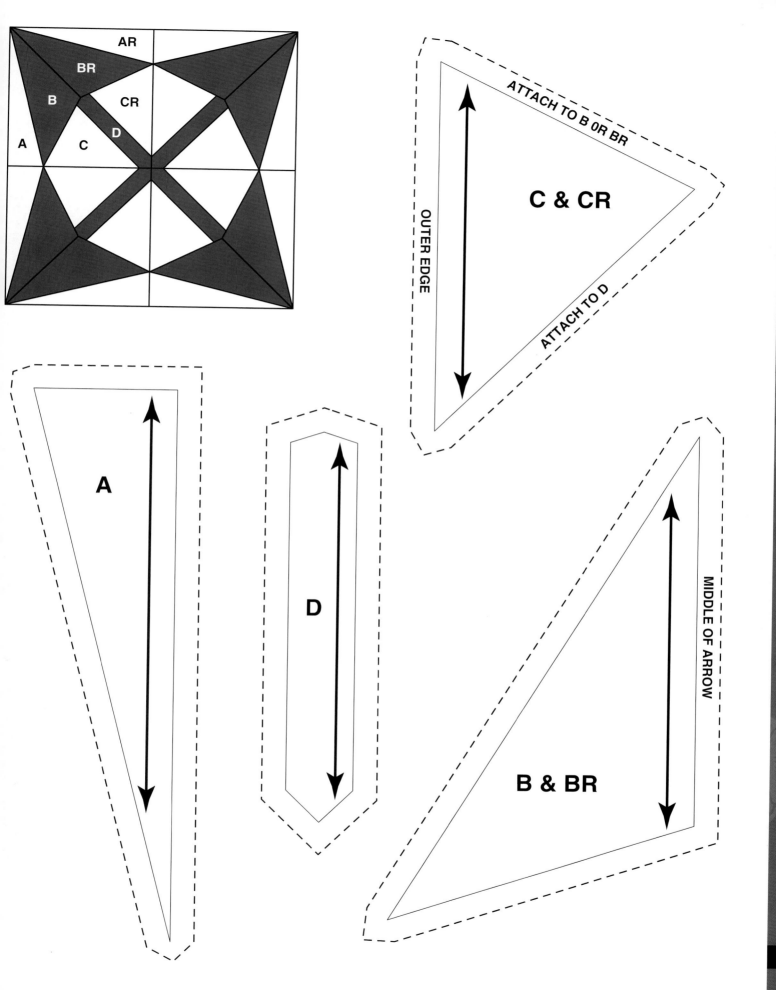

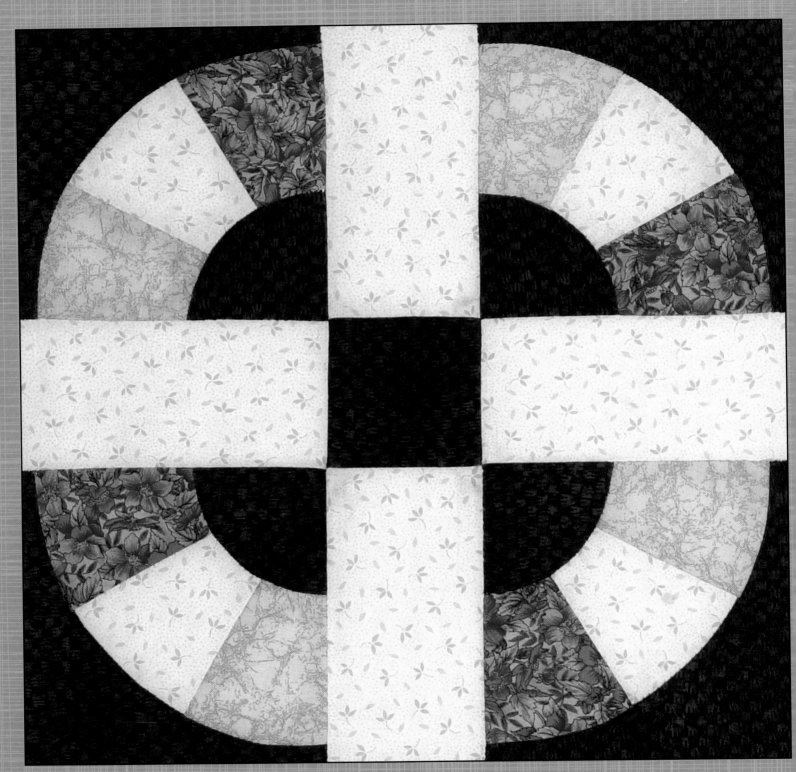

Around the World made by Shari McMillan of Marquette Heights, Illinois.

Lover's Lane

One August after suffering temperatures of more than 100 degrees for more than a month Casey, Michael, Joey and I headed north to Minnesota and Canada. Cooler climes were on our minds.

We planned to drive along the coast of Lake Superior on into Canada to see Fort William near Thunder Bay.

When we arrived at the lake we searched for a place to stay and found we could rent half of an A-frame cottage for a couple of nights. The clerk at the cottage was complaining about the heat. The high that day was 80 degrees and the boys and I were celebrating the cool air. I guess it's all a matter of perspective.

We unloaded our bags and got into our swimsuits. The boys all jumped into the lake at the same time. The water was icy c-c-c-cold. I dipped a toe in the water and quickly decided I'd watch from a boulder on the shore. When the boys' lips started to turn blue I made them get out of the water.

Later, we cooked hamburgers on the grill and watched the Canada geese waddle around in the yard. The boys tore up pieces of bread and fed them to the geese. We swung in a hammock and watched the geese squabble over pieces of bread the boys threw their way.

That night we started a fire in the fireplace, toasted marshmallows, and told ghost stories. The boys especially liked the gruesome tale of the couple who had been parked in a secluded lover's lane. The couple had kept the motor running so they could listen to music. A bulletin came over the radio telling everyone to be on the lookout for a one-armed man who had escaped from prison. The young man heard a noise, turned and saw a face peering in the window of the drivers' side of the car. He drove off as the intruder tried to open the car door. When they got to the girls' house, the story goes, the young man got out of his side of the car and saw a claw hook hanging from the door handle of the car.

Lover's Lane

12" Finished Block
1934

Fabric needed: light and dark.

From the light fabric, cut eight 2 1/2" squares (template A) and fourteen 2 7/8" squares. If you would rather used templates, cut 28 triangles using template B.

From the dark fabric, cut fourteen 2 7/8" squares. Again, if you would prefer to use templates, cut 28 triangles using template B.

You will need 28 half-square triangle units for the block. To make the half-square triangle units, draw a diagonal line from corner to corner on the reverse side of the light fabric.

Place a light square on top of a dark square with the right sides of the fabrics facing each other. Stitch 1/4" on either side of the diagonal line.

Cut the two pieces apart along the diagonal line, open each unit and press the seam allowance toward the dark side of the unit.

There are six rows in this block. Rows 1 and 6 are made in the same manner. Rows 2 and 5 are alike. Rows 3 and 4 are also alike.

To make rows 1 and 6, sew a half-square triangle to a light square.

Add four more half-square triangle units to complete the row as shown being careful with the placement of the dark portions. Remember, make two of these rows.

For rows 2 and 5, sew half-square triangles and squares together as shown.

For rows 3 and 4, sew the half-square triangles and squares together as shown.

To construct the block, sew row 1 and row 2 together as shown.

Now add row 3.

Rotate the remaining strips 180 degrees. Add row four.

Next add row 5.

Add row 6 to complete the block. It should look like this.

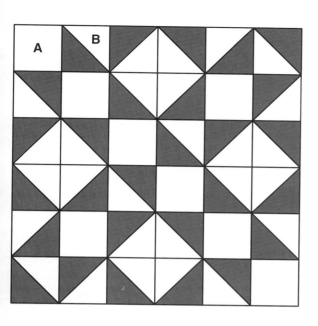

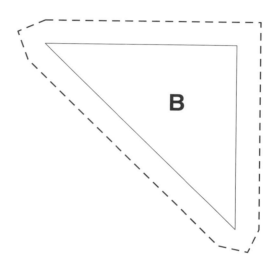

B

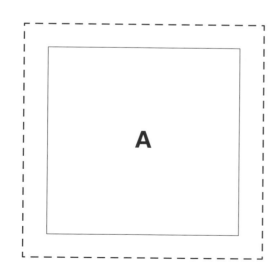

A

Many Roads to the White House made by Rosemary Garten of Independence, Missouri.

The Lake of the Ozarks winds all around the map of Missouri looking more like a river than a lake. That's probably because the lake really is a dammed up river. From Bagnell Dam to Osage Beach, it resembles a big S-curve then it trails off in a Westward direction. The lake is a popular playground for boaters, swimmers and fishing enthusiasts.

Casey learned to water ski at the lake. The boys' Aunt Cindy and Uncle Tom rented a condo one summer and invited us to join them. They brought their boat with them so we could enjoy skiing and tubing.

Tom was a good teacher. He actually got in the water with Casey on his shoulders and skied that way so that Casey would get the feeling of being pulled up out of the water. When it came time to put skis on Casey so he could try it himself, panic seized him and tears followed. Tom patiently took the skis off of Casey's feet, readjusted them and put them on his own feet. He then put Casey's feet in the boots on top of his own and off they went. Over and over, Tom and Casey were pulled up out of the water until Casey's fear was replaced with a big grin of accomplishment.

The quilt is old, it's edges frayed,

The colors faded dim.

He wraps it tight around his frame,

And feels her love for him.

K. C. STAR QUILTS!

VACATIONLAND

HAPPY DAYS ...ARE HERE

Ozark Trails
12" Finished Block
1933

Fabric needed: light, medium and dark.

From the light fabric, cut 4 triangles using template B, 8 triangles using template C, 8 triangles using template E and 8 triangles using template Er.

From the medium fabric, cut four 3 1/2" squares or use template B and one 4 3/4" square or use template F.

From the dark fabric, cut 8 triangles using template D.

Sew 2 light C pieces to a medium A piece as shown.

Make four of these A-C units.

Sew an E and Er piece to each side of a D triangle. This makes a rather squashed looking flying geese unit. Make 8 of these.

Sew two squashed geese to a corner A-C unit as shown. We'll call the end result corner posts. Make four of the corner posts.

Since this block is best constructed on the diagonal, sew a light B triangle to either side of a corner post. Make two of these sections.

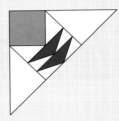

Now sew a corner post to opposing sides of the medium F square.

Sew the three sections together as shown to complete the block.

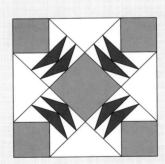

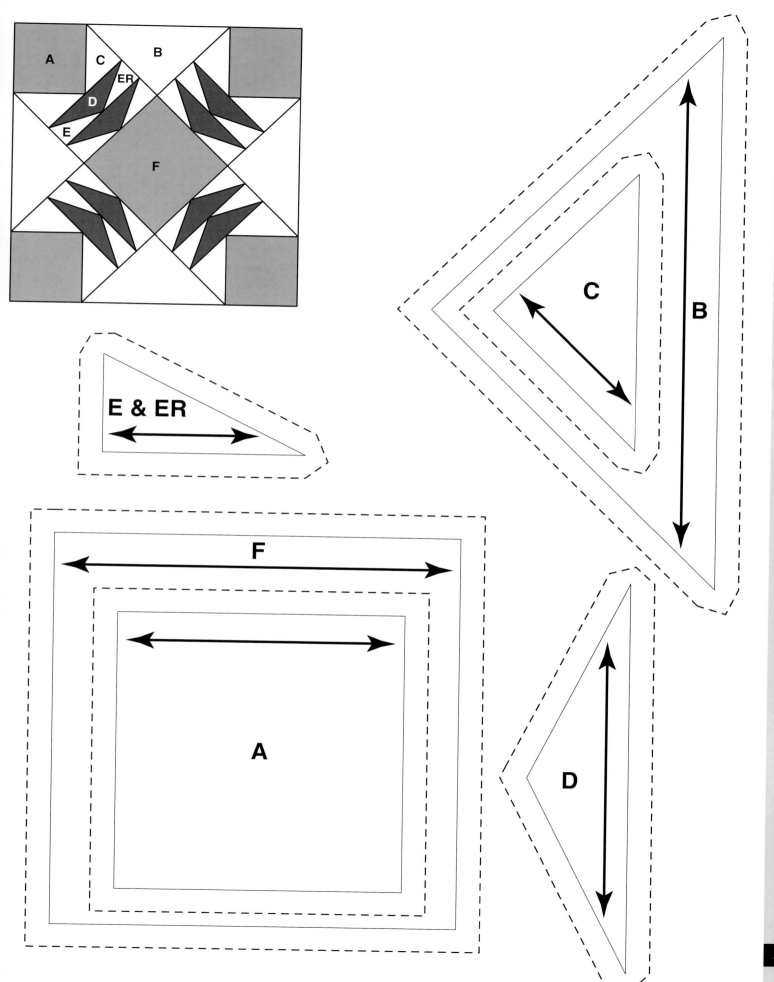

A

B

C

D

E & ER

F

Mountain Road made by Peggy McFeeters of Morton, Illinois.

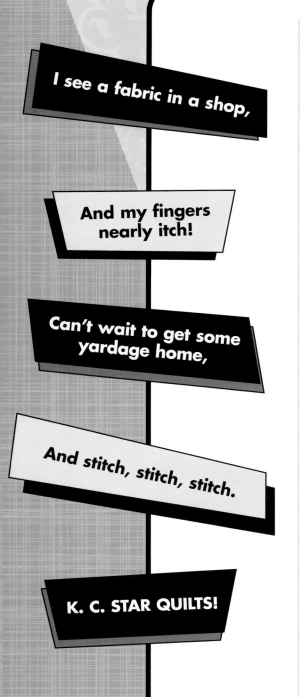

I see a fabric in a shop,

And my fingers nearly itch!

Can't wait to get some yardage home,

And stitch, stitch, stitch.

K. C. STAR QUILTS!

One of my favorite day trips from Kansas City is the jaunt to Jamesport, Missouri. Jamesport is primarily an Amish community. Horses and buggies are a common sight. Men in simple black coats and hats stare straight ahead, ignoring the "English," as they call us. The women visit with friends and neighbors while their children peep around their mommas' skirts and smile shyly.

The Amish are remarkable people. They work hard on their farms and work hard to hold on to their unique way of life. Amish women make incredible quilts, sewing by hand or on a treadle sewing machine like our grandmothers used to use. As a quilter, I can't begin to imagine life without my state-of-the-art sewing machine.

There are lots of antique shops in Jamesport. There is also a shop that sells hand made rugs and brooms. The owners are a married couple. He makes the brooms and she weaves the rugs on an old loom in the back of the shop. They have marvelous goods there. There is also an old-fashioned country store and a wonderful fabric shop.

The place my boys enjoyed most, however, was the restaurant and bakery. Directly over the bakery door is a large fan that vents the hot air that collects in the building. It also sends the heavenly aroma of freshly baked cinnamon rolls out onto the streets and sidewalks of town. Now that's good marketing! Not once have we ever left Jamesport without cinnamon rolls.

WE BUY AND SELL Antiques
A rare and interesting collection of unusual pieces..

Wagon Wheels Carry Me Home

12" Finished Block
1952

Fabric needed: light, medium and dark.

From the light fabric, cut six pieces using template B and one circle using template C.

From the medium fabric, cut four pieces using template A. You may want to cut the outside edges a bit larger than the template shows and trim and square the block when finished.

From the dark fabric, cut six pieces using template B.

Sew the light and dark B pieces together as shown. Leave the last seam open.

If you are piecing this block by hand, pin this to the center circle and stitch in place. Close the last seam. If you are machine piecing you might want to applique the circle in place.

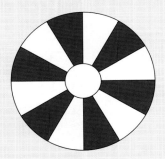

Add the medium outside corners to complete the block.

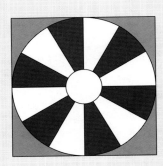

Square up and trim the block to 12 1/2."

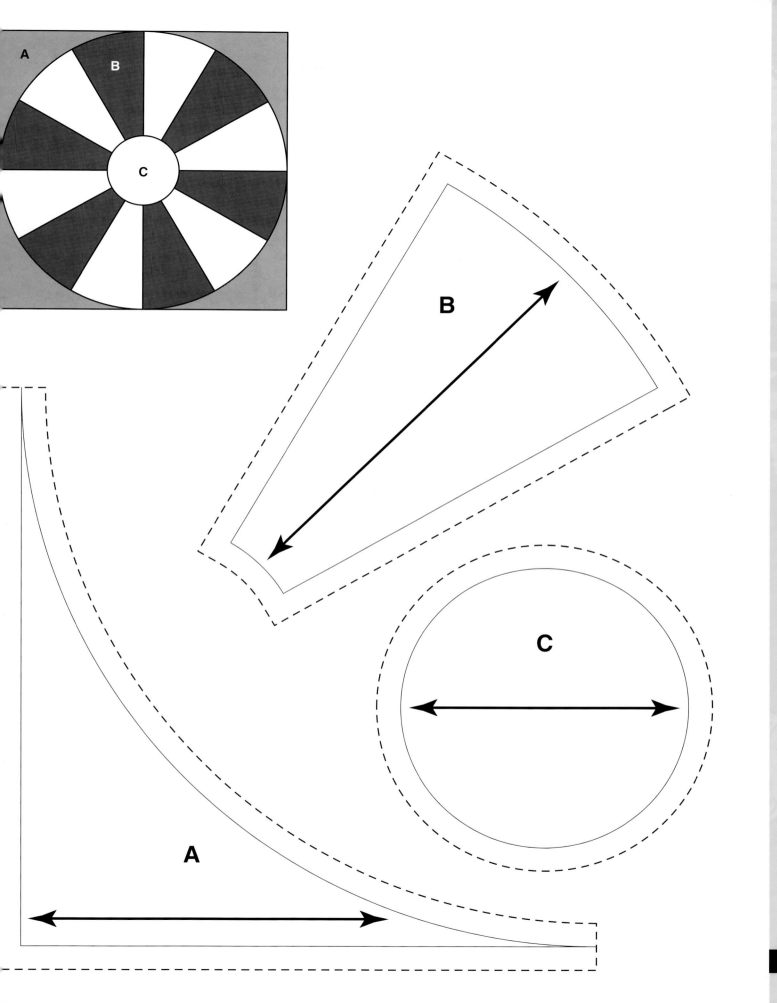

Car Wheel made by Corky Hutinett of Raytown, Missouri.

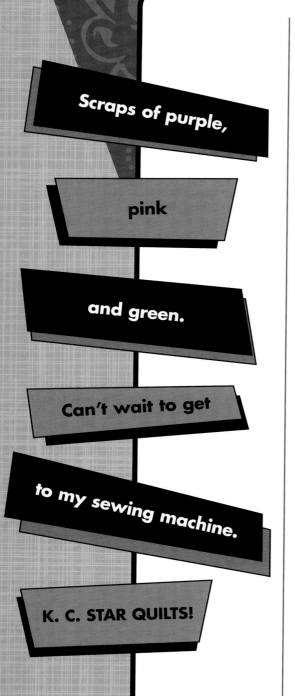

Scraps of purple,

pink

and green.

Can't wait to get

to my sewing machine.

K. C. STAR QUILTS!

Oklahoma has a rich heritage and history. It is a state filled with stories of Native Americans, pioneers, the land rush, oil, traders and cattle drives. Sadly enough it has had a sad chapter to add with the tragedy of the bombing of the Murrah building in Oklahoma City. The photo of the firefighter carrying a small child in his arms out of the rubble has been burned in my brain forever.

Oklahoma City has a strong quilt guild. In 1985 the guild began a project to collect and make all of the quilt patterns that had been published in The Kansas City Star. As the blocks were completed they were mounted on panels covered in black felt. The last blocks were completed in 1989.

The panels were shown in conjunction with a quilt show held at Bartle Hall in Kansas City. It was an international exhibit and all the quilts shown had been juried in. One of the categories was Kansas City Star quilts.

I entered a pinwheel quilt made from feedsacks I had collected. The pinwheels were made from printed feedsacks and the back contained white sacks that still had the logos visible.

I dragged all three of my boys to the show after the judging had taken place. Reluctantly I went to view my own quilt certain it couldn't have been good enough to win anything. As we neared the quilt I could see a ribbon hanging on the edge. I grabbed Joe by the arm and said, "Oh my gosh, oh my gosh, there's a ribbon on it! I can't believe it, there's a ribbon on it!"

Joe stopped me and looked at me and said, "Mom, I'm really glad there's a ribbon on it but would you please not grab my arm again. I think I could be getting some bruises here."

Road to Oklahoma

12" Finished Block
1957

Fabric needed: light, medium and dark.

From the light fabric, cut four 2 1/2" squares or use template E and four pieces using template B and four pieces using template Br. If you fold your fabric and cut through both layers at once using template B, you will then have the Br pieces you need.

From the medium fabric, cut four triangles using template C.

From the dark fabric, cut four pieces using template A and five 2 1/2" squares or use template E.

Make the center 9-patch unit first by sewing a dark square to either side of a light square. Make two rows that look like this.

Now sew a light square to either side of a dark square.

Next sew the three rows together to complete the 9-patch center.

It should look like this.

Now add a medium C triangle to each side of the 9-patch unit.

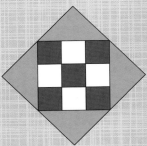

Sew the corner units together by sewing a light Br piece to a dark A piece. Add a light B piece to the opposing side of the dark A piece. Make four of these corner units.

Sew the corner units to the center as shown to complete the block.

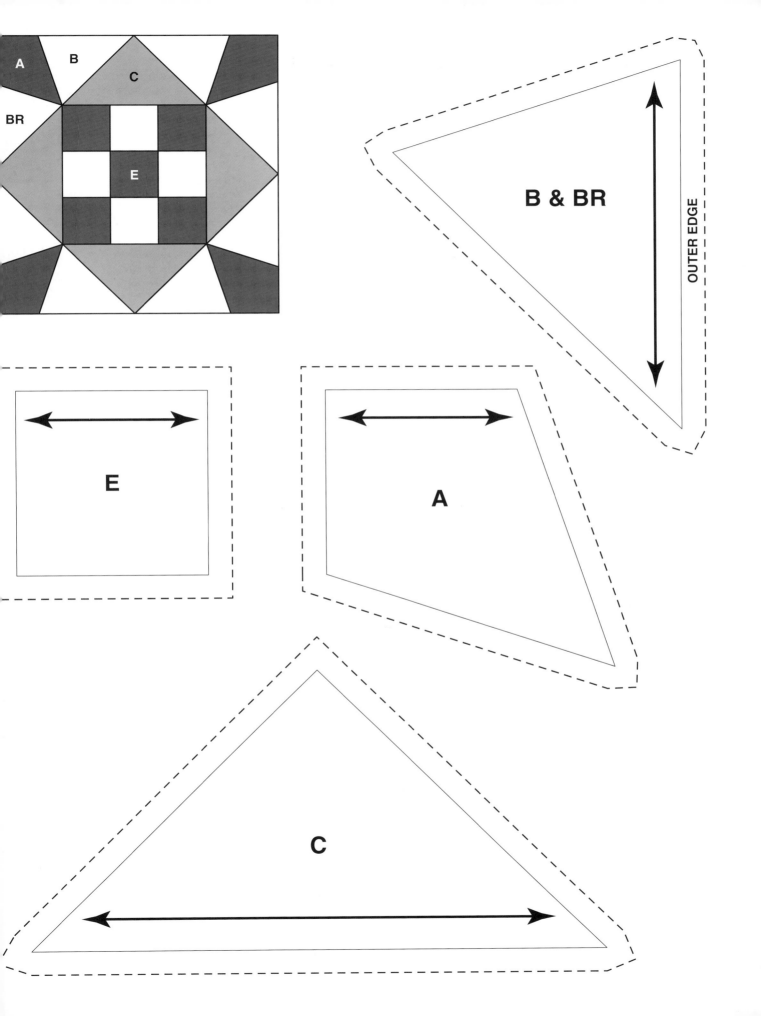

B & BR

OUTER EDGE

E

A

C

Bridle Path made by Ruby Downing of Oak Grove, Missouri.

Roads to Berlin

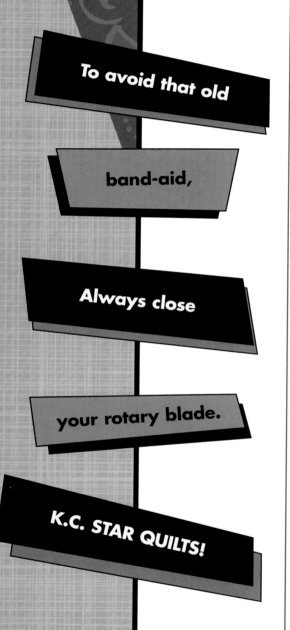

To avoid that old band-aid, Always close your rotary blade.

K.C. STAR QUILTS!

My son, Michael and his fiancé, Sarah Walker, attended Illinois College in Jacksonville, Illinois. While studying foreign languages, they had the opportunity to visit Germany.

While there, Michael, Sarah, and eight other students were in a little pub in Berlin. The decor was dark and there were candles on the tables, creating a cozy atmosphere.

When it was time to order drinks, the waitress leaned over Sarah's shoulder to ask what she wanted. Suddenly the waitress shrieked, "Scheissen! Scheissen!" and the distinct odor of singed hair filled the little room. It seems the waitress had leaned too close to the candle and the flame had ignited her hairspray.

The waitress ran off to put out the flames, but returned a few minutes later to get the rest of the drink orders. At the end of the evening, the group left her a sizeable tip. After all, she was one HOT waitress.

BEER! with YOUR LUNCH

NOT ONLY GOOD - BUT GOOD FOR YOU

Roads to Berlin

12" Finished Block
1944

Fabric needed: light, medium and dark.

From the light fabric, cut four 3 1/2" squares.

From the medium fabric, cut 16 triangles using template B.

From the dark fabric, cut 16 parallelograms using template A.

Sew a medium B triangle to a dark A parallelogram. You will need to make 16 of these units.

Add a parallelogram unit to the top and bottom of the light square.

Now add a parallelogram unit to each side of the light square. This completes one-fourth of the block.

Make three more of these squares.

Sew the four squares together as shown to complete the block.

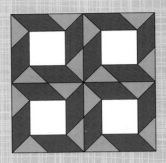

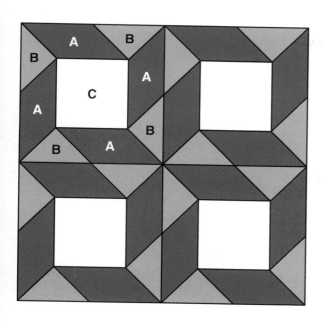

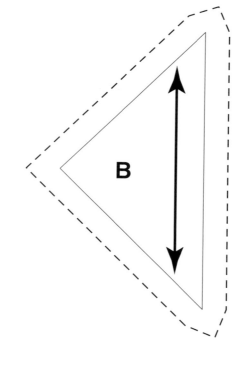

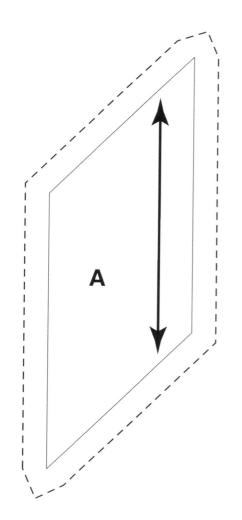

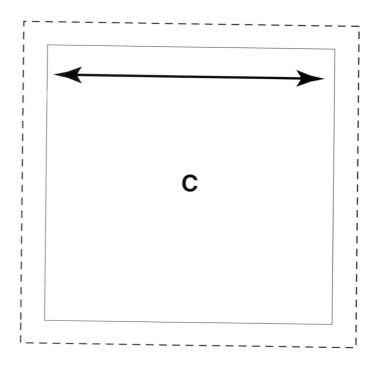

End of the Road made by Viv Browning of Peoria, Illinois.

My boys are all grown up now and they plan their own vacations. I no longer have to worry about them missing school if I have take time off work during the school year. I'll never again look in my rearview mirror to see Joey falling asleep as I back out of the driveway. No more will I have to find the first available restroom before we leave Kansas City because Michael has had too much soda. Casey won't be chattering a mile a minute or doing a poor imitation of a rapper. No one yells, "I get the front seat by the window."

On the other hand, they aren't tortured with visits to quilt shops and museums that just "happen" to be having a quilt show. They no longer have to pretend to enjoy selecting fabric or "oooh" and "aaaah" over my choices. They no longer have to endure Neil Diamond tapes playing constantly on the tape deck. They don't have to listen to me yell, "Don't make me stop this car!"

Since the boys are grown, my destinations have changed for vacations. Now I travel to Paducah every year to see the American Quilter's Society quilt show. I travel to California to visit my friends and my nephew, Ken and his wife, Barb. I visit Houston every year for Quilt Market. Technically that is a business trip but is entirely too much fun for me to call work.

Most of our vacations were taken on a shoestring budget, but what fun we had. I can't think of one day I would have missed or traded. The memories I share with these young men are priceless to me. I hope they feel the same and pass on the vacation tradition to their own families.

Like every parent, I wish for the roads in their lives to be smooth and for the curves ahead of them to hold pleasant surprises.

I've lived my life the best I can

So if my legacy

Is all the quilts that I have made

Then they'll speak well for me.

K. C. STAR QUILTS!

119

End of the Road

12" Finished Block
1952

Fabric needed: light, dark and medium.

From the light fabric, cut one 6 1/2" x 2 1/2" strip or use template B and two triangles using template A.

From the medium fabric, cut one 6 1/2" x 2 1/2" strip or use template B and four triangles using template A.

From the dark fabric, cut one 6 1/2" x 2 1/2" strip or use template B and six triangles using template A.

Sew the three strips together with the medium strip on top and the dark fabric on the bottom.

Add a light A triangle to the top and the bottom of the square you have just made.

Add a dark A triangle to opposing sides of the square as shown.

Now sew a dark and a medium A triangle together to make a corner unit. Make a total of four corner units.

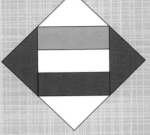

To complete the block, add the corner units as shown.

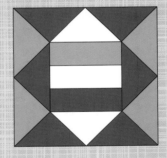

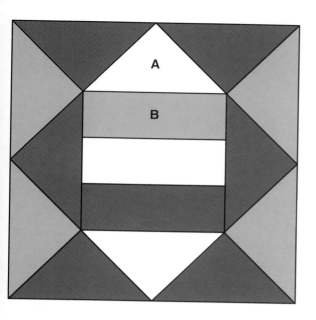

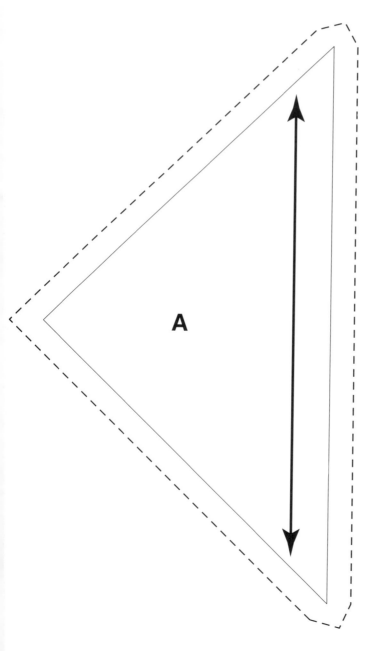

A

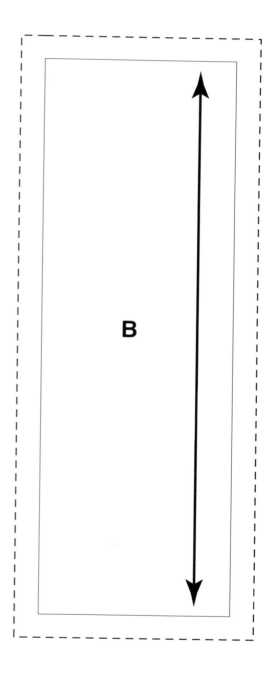

B

Putting it all Together

These instructions are for setting the blocks together on point. The sashing strips and cornerstones are two inches wide when finished. This type of setting required twenty-five blocks so I made another "Road to Arkansas" block and used them in opposing corners. After adding a two-inch framing border and a four-inch outside border, the quilt measured 94 inches square.

The four corner triangles are made by cutting two squares in half at a 45-degree angle, corner to corner. To determine the size of the square needed, divide the finished block size by 1.414 and add .875" for the seam allowances. For example, if the finished block size measures 12," the formula would look like this:

$$12'' \div 1.414 = 8.48 + .875 = 9.355$$

Round this figure up to the nearest 1/8th inch and you have a square of 9 3/8."

To make the side triangles, cut a square in quarters. Cut at a forty-five degree angle from corner to corner twice. Each square will make four triangles. To determine the size of the square, multiply the finished block size by 1.414 and add 1.25 and round the number up to the nearest eighth.

$$12'' \times 1.414 = 16.96'' + 1.25 = 18.20''$$

Round this up to 18.25" and cut as directed above.

If you are using sashing, be sure to consider that measurement in your finished block size. By using these cutting directions, the straight of grain of your fabric will always be on the outside edges of the quilt, thus making it easier to add borders.